Book Three

Native Americans • North America • The Pilgrims

Draw • Write • NOW®

by
Marie Hablitzel
and
Kim Stitzer

*A Drawing
and Handwriting
Course for Kids!*

Barker Creek Publishing, Inc. • Poulsbo, Washington

Dedicated to...

...my grandchildren.
I have enjoyed drawing with you! — M.H.

...Tyler's teachers — Debra Manos, Kathleen Wright Davalos and Jill Spring Hayes — K.S.

The authors thank the following for their contributions to this book:
Linda Owen, Indian Education Coordinator for the Bremerton, Washington School District and Edward Patrick Hogan,
South Dakota State Geographer, South Dakota State University, Brookings, South Dakota for their assistance and guidance.
The Dallas Museum of Art for granting permission to draw the Anasazi pottery on page 32. The pottery is part of the museum's
Foundation for the Arts collection, anonymous gift, object number 1991.336.FA.
The TSA-LA-GI Cultural Center in Tahlequah, Oklahoma, for translating "Handwriting is an Ancient Art"
on page 8 into the Cherokee Sylabary.

The text on the handwriting pages is set in a custom
font created from Marie Hablitzel's handwriting.
The drawings are done using Berol Prismacolor pencils
outlined with a black PaperMate FLAIR!® felt tip pen.

BARKER CREEK

Published by Barker Creek Publishing, Inc.
P.O. Box 2610 • Poulsbo, WA 98370-2610
800•692•5833 FAX: 360•613•2542
www.barkercreek.com

Text and Illustration Copyright © 1996 by Kim Hablitzel Stitzer

Book layout by Judy Richardson
Computer graphics by Jeanne Doran
Printed in Hong Kong

Library of Congress Catalog Card Number: 93-73893
Publisher's Cataloging in Publication Data:
Hablitzel, Marie, 1920 -
Draw•Write•Now®, Book Three: A drawing and handwriting course for kids!
(third in series)

Summary: A collection of drawing and handwriting lessons for children. *Book Three* focuses on Native Americans, North America and The Pilgrims. Third book in the *Draw•Write•Now®* series.

1. Drawing — Technique — Juvenile Literature. 2. Drawing — Study and Teaching (Elementary). 3. Penmanship. 4. Indians of North America — Juvenile Literature. 5. Geography — Juvenile Literature. 6. Pilgrims (New Plymouth Colony) — Juvenile Literature.
I. Stitzer, Kim, 1956 -   , coauthor. II. Title.
741.2   [372.6]

ISBN: 0-9639307-3-7

Fourth Printing

About this book...

For most children, drawing is their first form of written communication. Long before they master the alphabet and sentence syntax, children express themselves creatively on paper through line and color.

As children mature, their imaginations often race ahead of their drawing skills. By teaching them to see complex objects as combinations of simple shapes and encouraging them to develop their fine-motor skills through regular practice, they can better record the images they see so clearly in their minds.

This book contains a collection of beginning drawing lessons and text for practicing handwriting. These lessons were developed by a teacher who saw her second-grade students becoming increasingly frustrated with their drawing efforts and disenchanted with repetitive handwriting drills.

For more than 30 years, Marie Hablitzel refined what eventually became a daily drawing and handwriting curriculum. Marie's premise was simple —drawing and handwriting require many of the same skills. And, regular practice in a supportive environment is the key to helping children develop

*Coauthors Marie Hablitzel (left)
and her daughter, Kim Stitzer*

their technical skills, self-confidence and creativity. As a classroom teacher, Marie intertwined her daily drawing and handwriting lessons with math, science, social studies, geography, reading and creative writing. She wove an educational tapestry that hundreds of children have found challenging, motivating — and fun!

Although Marie is now retired, her drawing and handwriting lessons continue to be used in the classroom. With the assistance of her daughter, Kim Stitzer, Marie shares more than 150 of her lessons in the eight-volume *Draw•Write•Now®* series.

In *Draw•Write•Now®, Book One,* children explore life on a farm, kids and critters and storybook characters. *Books Two* through *Six* feature topics as diverse as Christopher Columbus, the weather, Native Americans, the polar regions, young Abraham Lincoln, beaver ponds and life in the sea. In *Draw•Write•Now®, Books Seven and Eight,* children circle the globe while learning about animals of the world.

We hope your children and students enjoy these lessons as much as ours have!

—*Carolyn Hurst, Publisher*

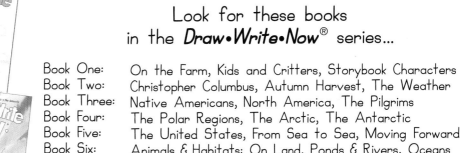

Look for these books in the *Draw•Write•Now®* series...

Book One: On the Farm, Kids and Critters, Storybook Characters
Book Two: Christopher Columbus, Autumn Harvest, The Weather
Book Three: Native Americans, North America, The Pilgrims
Book Four: The Polar Regions, The Arctic, The Antarctic
Book Five: The United States, From Sea to Sea, Moving Forward
Book Six: Animals & Habitats: On Land, Ponds & Rivers, Oceans
Book Seven: Animals of the World, Part I
Book Eight: Animals of the World, Part II

...coming soon from Barker Creek Publishing
For additional information call 1-800-692-5833
or visit our website at www.barkercreek.com

Table of Contents

A table of contents is like a map. It guides you to the places you want to visit in a book. Pick a subject you want to draw, then turn to the page listed beside the picture.

For more information on the *Draw•Write•Now*® series, see page 3. For suggestions on how to use this book, see page 6. For a review of handwriting tips, see page 8.

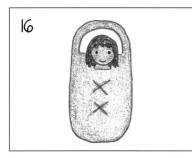

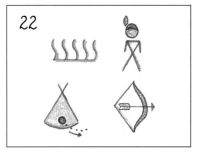
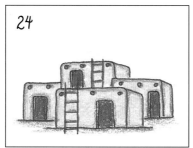

North America   Page 35

The Pilgrims   Page 49

Teaching Tips   Page 63

A few tips to get started...

This is a book for children and their parents, teachers and caregivers. Although most young people can complete the lessons in this book quite successfully on their own, a little help and encouragement from a caring adult can go a long way toward building a child's self-confidence, creativity and technical skills.

Young Abe Lincoln by John Trent, age 9
from Draw•Write•Now®, Book Five

The following outline contains insights from the 30-plus years the authors have worked with the material in this book. Realizing that no two children or classrooms are alike, the authors encourage you to modify these lessons to best suit the needs of your child or classroom. Each Draw•Write•Now® lesson includes five parts:

1. Introduce the subject.
2. Draw the subject.
3. Draw the background.
4. Practice handwriting.
5. Color the drawing.

As presented here, each child will need a pencil, an eraser, drawing paper, penmanship paper and either crayons, color pencils or felt tip markers to complete a lesson.

1. Introduce the Subject

Begin the lesson by generating interest in the subject with a story, discussion, poem, photograph or song. The questions on the illustrated notes scattered throughout this book are examples of how interest can be built along a related theme. Answers to these questions and the titles of several theme-related books are on pages 34, 48 and 62.

2. Draw the Subject

Have the children draw with a pencil. Encourage them to draw lightly because some lines (shown as dashed lines on the drawing lessons) may need to be erased. Show the children the finished drawing in the book. Point out the shapes and lines in the subject as the children work through the lesson. Help the children see that complex objects can be viewed as combinations of lines and simple shapes.

Help the children be successful! Show them how to position the first step on their papers in an appropriate size. Initially, the children may find some shapes difficult to draw. If they do, provide a pattern for them to trace, or draw the first step for them. Once they fine-tune their skills and build their self-confidence, their ability and creativity will take over. For lesson-specific drawing tips and suggestions, refer to *Teaching Tips* on pages 63–64.

3. Draw the Background

Encourage the children to express their creativity and imagination in the backgrounds they add to their pictures. Add to their creative libraries by demonstrating various ways to draw trees, horizons and other details. Point out background details in the drawings in this book, illustrations from other books, photographs and works of art.

Encourage the children to draw their world by looking for basic shapes and lines in the things they see around them. Ask them to draw from their imaginations by using their developing skills. For additional ideas on motivating children to draw creatively, see pages 32–33, 46–47 and 60–61.

4. Practice Handwriting

In place of drills — rows of e's, r's and so on — it is often useful and more motivating to have children write complete sentences when practicing their handwriting. When the focus is on handwriting —

rather than spelling or vocabulary enrichment — use simple words that the children can easily read and spell. Begin by writing each word with the children, demonstrating how individual letters are formed and stressing proper spacing. Start slowly. One or two sentences may be challenging enough in the beginning. Once the children are consistently forming their letters correctly, encourage them to work at their own pace.

There are many ways to adapt these lessons for use with your child or classroom. For example, you may want to replace the authors' text with your own words. You may want to let the children compose sentences to describe their drawings or answer the theme-related questions found throughout the book. You may prefer to replace the block alphabet used in this book with a cursive, D'Nealian® or other alphabet style. If you are unfamiliar with the various alphabet styles used for teaching handwriting, consult your local library. A local elementary school may also be able to recommend an appropriate alphabet style and related resource materials.

5. Color the Picture

Children enjoy coloring their own drawings. The beautiful colors, however, often cover the details they have so carefully drawn in pencil. To preserve their efforts, you may want to have the children trace their pencil lines with black crayons or fine-tipped felt markers.

Crayons — When coloring with crayons, have the children outline their drawings with a black crayon *after* they have colored their pictures (the

Racoon by Kara Ryan, age 7
from Draw•Write•Now®, Book Eight

Mount Vernon by Eric Brown, age 7
from Draw•Write•Now®, Book Five

black crayon may smear if they do their outlining first).

Color Pencils—When coloring with color pencils, have the children outline their drawings with a felt tip marker *before* they color their drawings.

Felt Tip Markers—When coloring with felt tip markers, have the children outline their drawings with a black marker *after* they have colored their pictures.

Your comments are appreciated!
    The authors would appreciate hearing from you. Write to Marie Hablitzel and Kim Stitzer, c/o Barker Creek Publishing, Inc., P.O. Box 2610, Poulsbo, WA 98370, USA or visit our website at www.barkercreek.com.

Duck by Kiah Vande Putte, age 5
from Draw•Write•Now®, Book One

ᎠᏍᏗ ᎠᏚᎮᏟ ᏗᏣᎦᏜᏫᎤᏐᏗᏍᎢ*

Learn about the Nations shown on this map on pages 9-34

Haida

Ojibway

Wintun

Lakota

Iroquois

Hopi

Cherokee

Petroglyph from
Connecticut River, Vermont

Petroglyph from
Noeick River, British Columbia

The more you practice, the better your handwriting will look!

Petroglyph from
Largo Canyon, New Mexico

Petroglyph from
Three Rivers, New Mexico

*Handwriting is an Ancient Art!

Translation into the Cherokee Sylabary
courtesy of the Cherokee Cultural Center in Tahlequah, Oklahoma

Native Americans

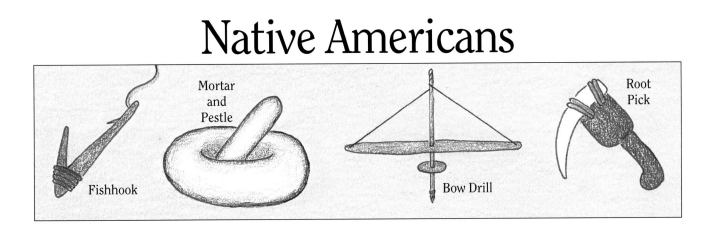

Fishhook

Mortar and Pestle

Bow Drill

Root Pick

The Ojibway lived in forests.
There were rivers and lakes.
They traveled in canoes.
Their canoes were made of bark.

What is special about birch bark canoes?

Birch Bark Canoe

Question answered on page 34

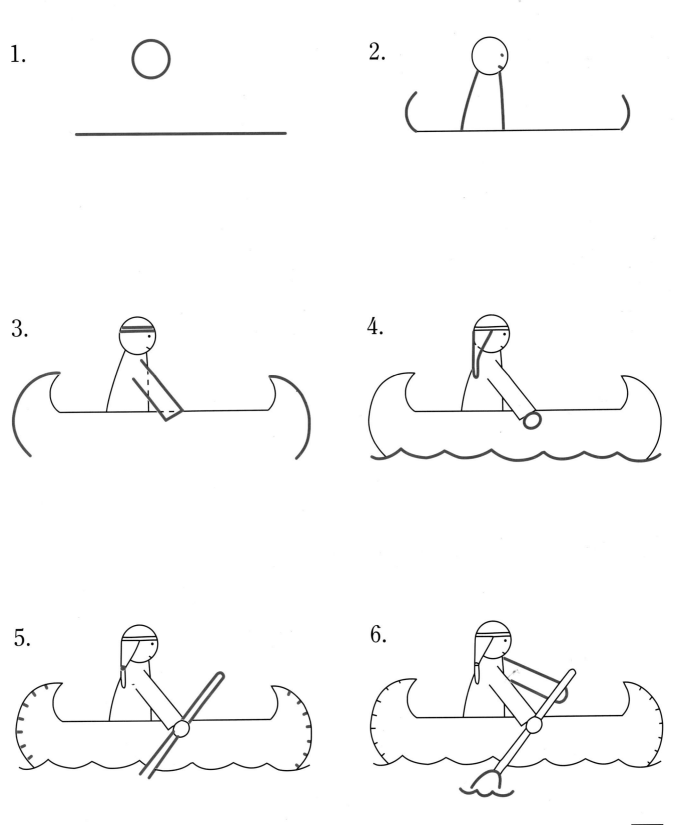

1.

2.

3.

4.

5.

6.

Longhouse

Question answered on page 34

1.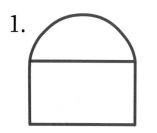

2.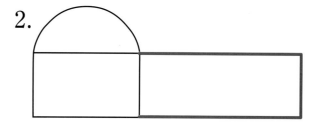

3.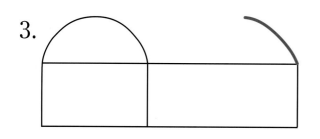

4.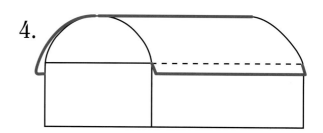

5.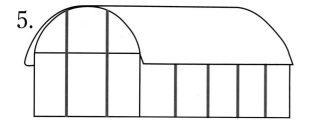

6.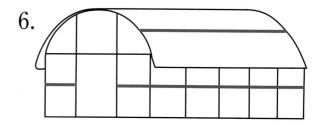

7.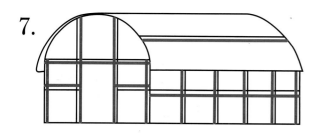

8.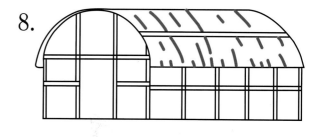

The Iroquois built bark houses.
Some were very large.
They were called longhouses.
Many families lived in them.

How many families lived in a longhouse?

The Cherokee were hunters.
They were also farmers.
They lived in wooded valleys.
Mountains surrounded them.

Do the Cherokee still live in the wooded valleys of their ancestors?

Question answered on page 34

1.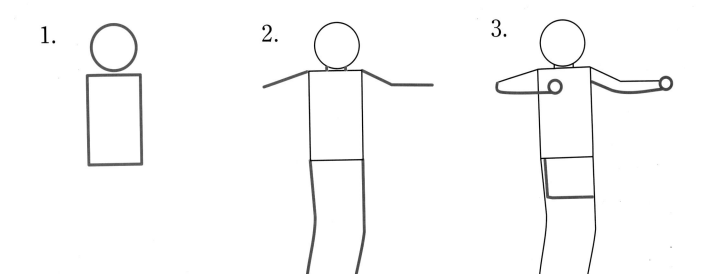

2.

3.

4.

5.

6.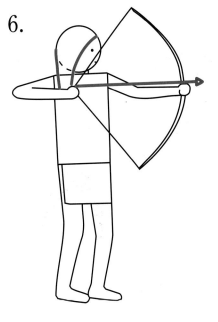

Cradleboard

Question answered on page 34

1.

2.

3.

4.

5.

6.

Nez Perce

Hupa

Apache

Cherokee

Mothers had many chores.
Their babies stayed nearby.
Babies lay in cradleboards.
Mothers kept close watch.

How are cradleboards used?

The Lakota lived on the plains.
They moved often.
Their homes were tepees.
Tepees were easy to move.

What other people are from the plains?

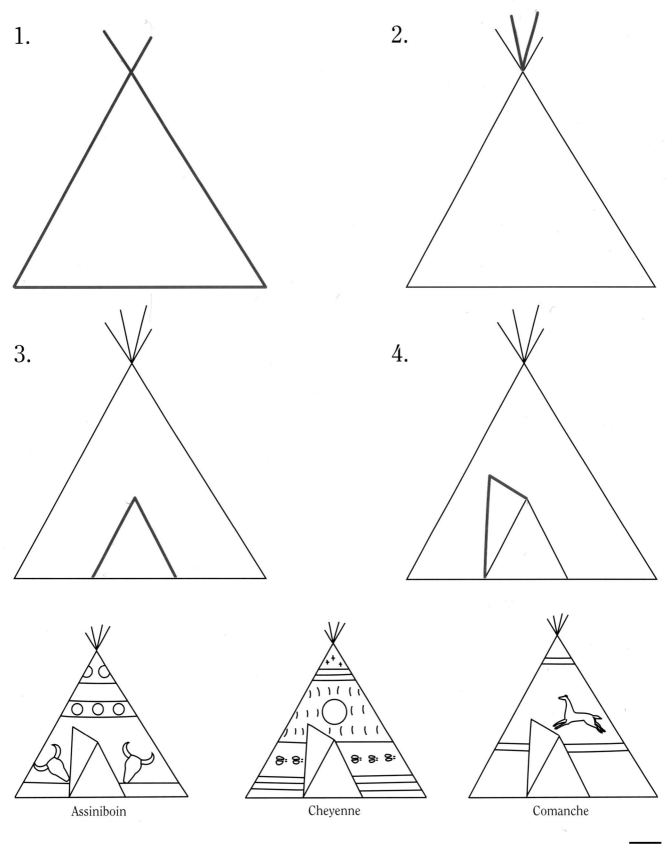

1.

2.

3.

4.

Assiniboin

Cheyenne

Comanche

Bison

Question answered on page 34

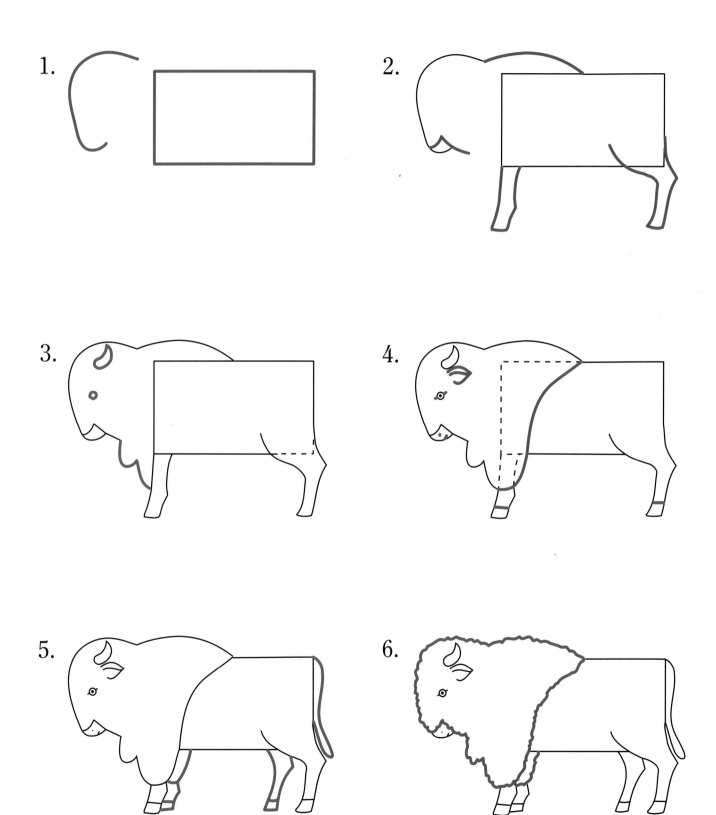

Bison lived on the plains.
Their herds were huge.
They roamed long distances.
People hunted the bison.

What is another name for bison?

People wrote with pictures.
Some drew on bison hides.
A hide was like a book.
Each hide told a story.

Where can
you see
picture
writing?

Picture Writing

Question answered on page 34

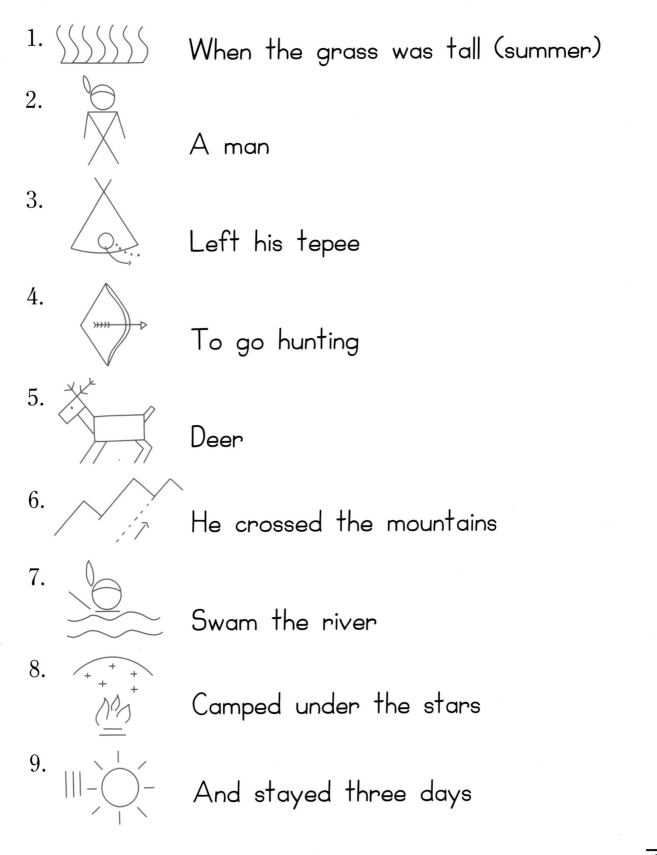

1. When the grass was tall (summer)

2. A man

3. Left his tepee

4. To go hunting

5. Deer

6. He crossed the mountains

7. Swam the river

8. Camped under the stars

9. And stayed three days

Pueblo

Teaching Tip on page 64
Question answered on page 34

1.

2.

3.

4.

5.

6.

7.

8.

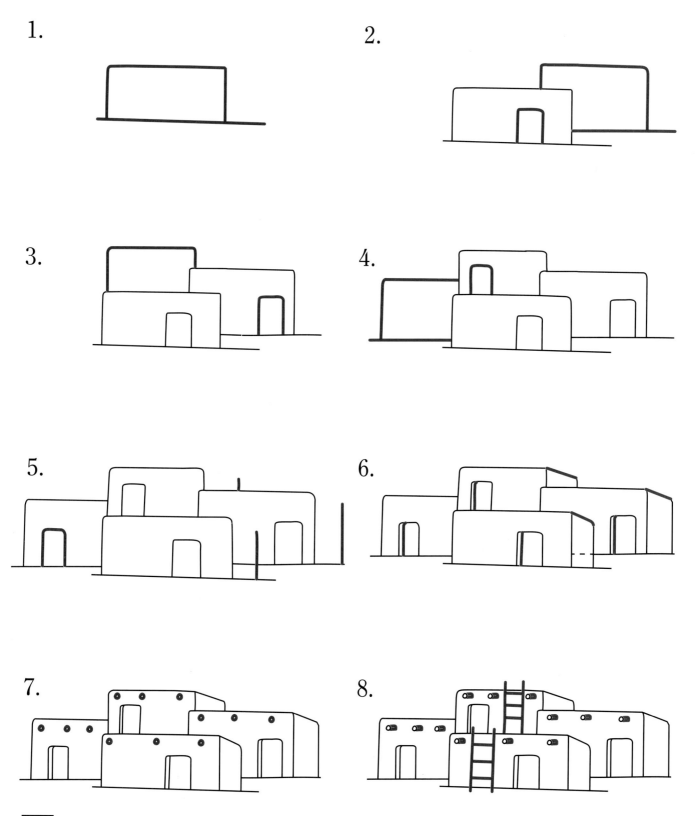

The Hopi lived in pueblos.
Pueblos had several rooms.
Many families lived together.
A pueblo was like an apartment.

What is the oldest town in the United States?

Some places had clay.
The people made beautiful pots.
Other people made baskets.
They used bark or reeds.

Why does
Chippewa art
differ from
Zuni art?

Pots and Baskets

Teaching Tip on Page 64
Question answered on page 34

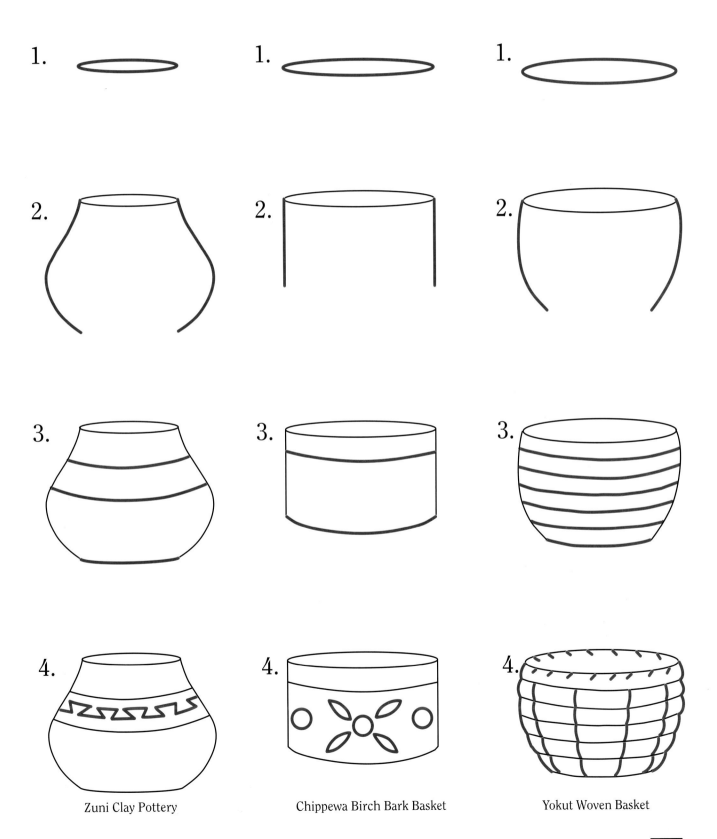

1.

2.

3.

4.

Zuni Clay Pottery

1.

2.

3.

4.

Chippewa Birch Bark Basket

1.

2.

3.

4.

Yokut Woven Basket

Gatherer

Question answered on page 34

1.

2.

3.

4.

5.

6.

The Wintun lived in a valley.
The weather was mild.
Food was plentiful.
They gathered acorns.

Where is the Wintun's valley?

The Haida lived by the ocean.
Salmon swam in the rivers.
The Haida fished.
They carved totem poles.

How are
totem poles
like picture
writing?

Totem Pole

Question answered on page 34

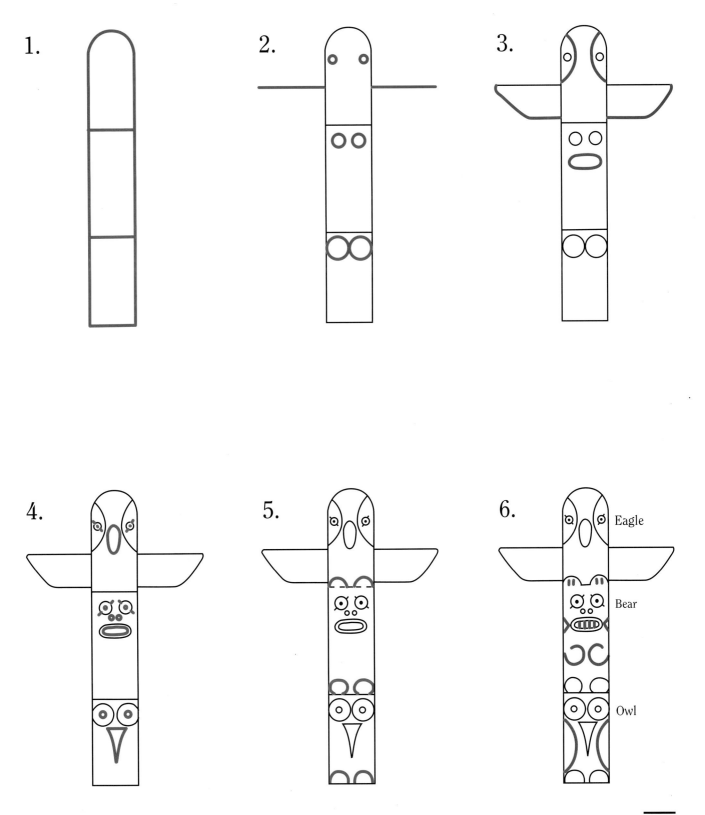

1.

2.

3.

4.

5.

6.   Eagle

Bear

Owl

Draw What You See

Do you see drawings on...

Rocks?

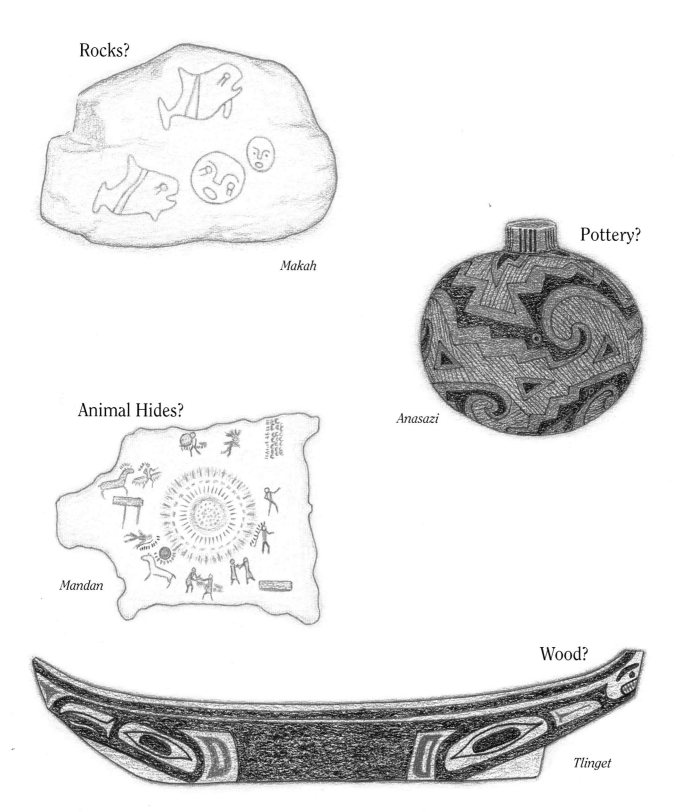

Makah

Pottery?

Anasazi

Animal Hides?

Mandan

Wood?

Tlinget

Creating colors from nature...

Paints, dyes and pottery glazes can be made from plants and minerals.

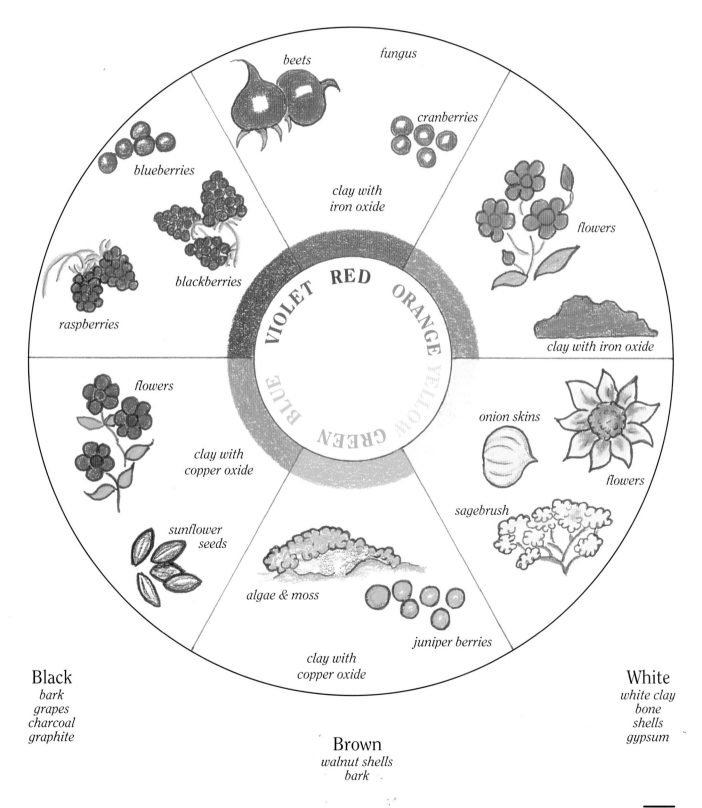

Learn more about Native Americans...

North America

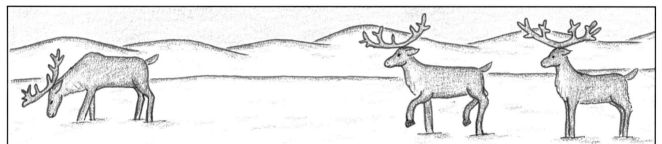

The East has mountains.
It has many kinds of trees.
The East has lowlands, too.
They border the Atlantic.

How do farms and cities affect forests?

Question answered on page 48

Deer

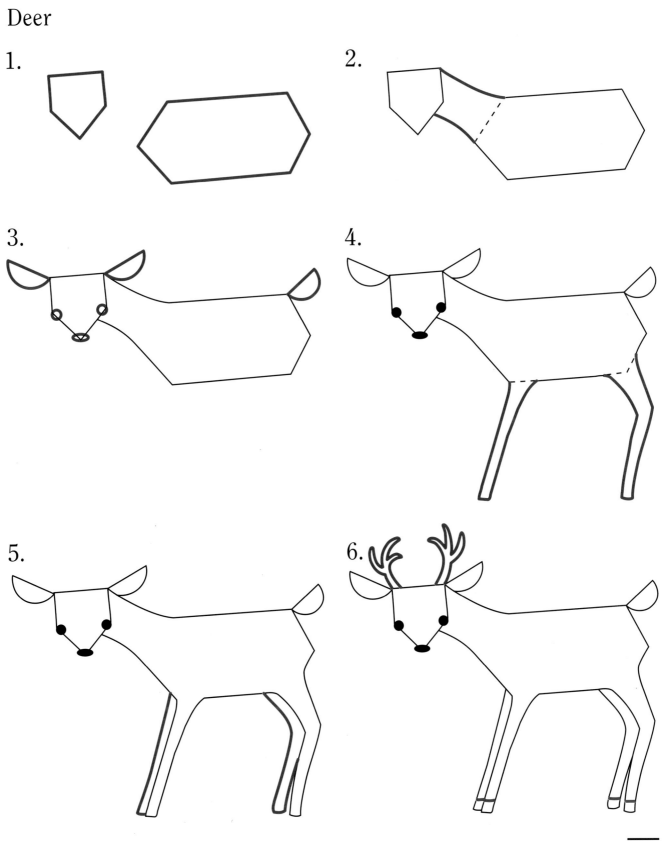

1.

2.

3.

4.

5.

6.

The Interior

Teaching Tip on page 64
Question answered on page 48

Sunflower

1.

2.

3.

4.

5.

6.

The Interior is mostly flat.

It has fertile plains.

Grasses once covered the plains.

Wildflowers grow here.

What other plants grow in the Interior?

The West has tall mountains.
The Rockies are the largest.
It has basins and plateaus.
It also has many valleys.

Can you find the mountain ranges of North America on a map?

Teaching Tip on page 64
Question answered on page 48

Eagle

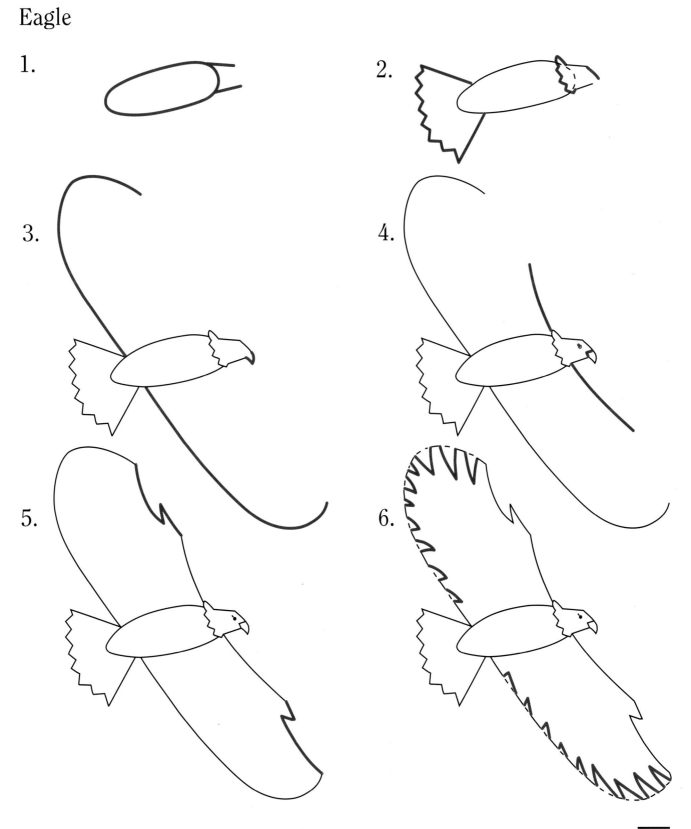

The South

Question answered on page 48

Saguaro Cactus

1.

2.

Prickly Pear Cactus

1.

2.

3.

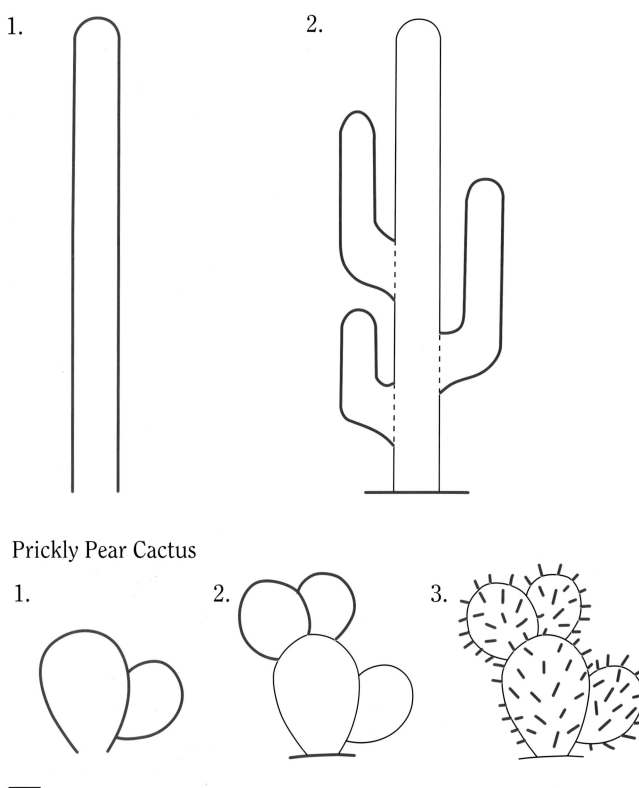

It is hot in the South.

Some areas get a lot of rain.

Other areas are dry deserts.

Cacti grow here.

What happens when it rains on the desert?

Northern winters are cold.
Summers can seem very short.
Forests give way to tundra.
Many animals live here.

What is the tundra?

Question answered on page 48

Caribou

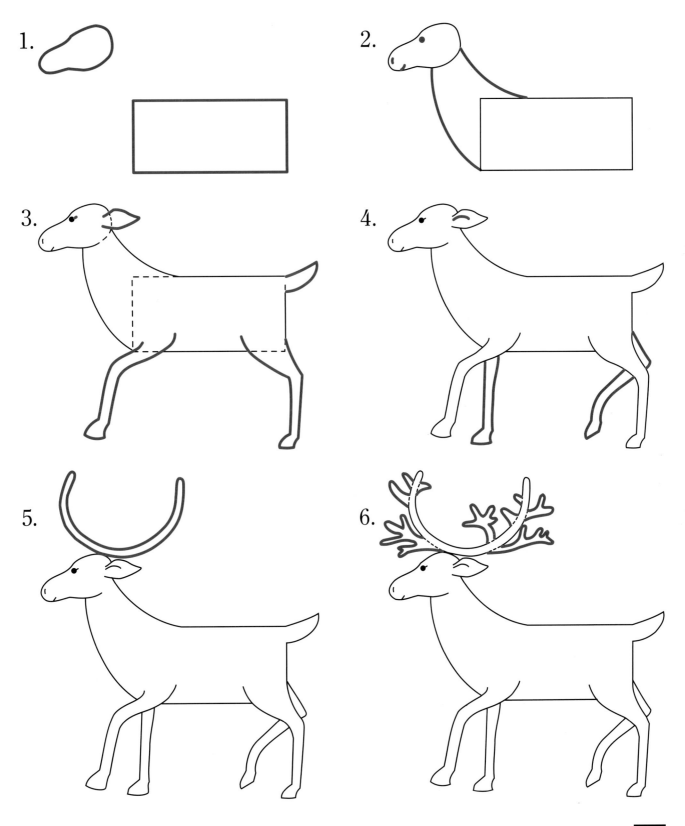

1.

2.

3.

4.

5.

6.

Draw Your World

Where do you live? What colors do you see?

Reds?

Yellows?

Blues?

Red, yellow and blue are the "primary" colors.

With these three colors, you can make all the colors of the rainbow!

Orange, green and violet are the "secondary" colors.

Secondary colors are made by mixing two primary colors.

red + yellow = orange

yellow + blue = green

blue + red = violet

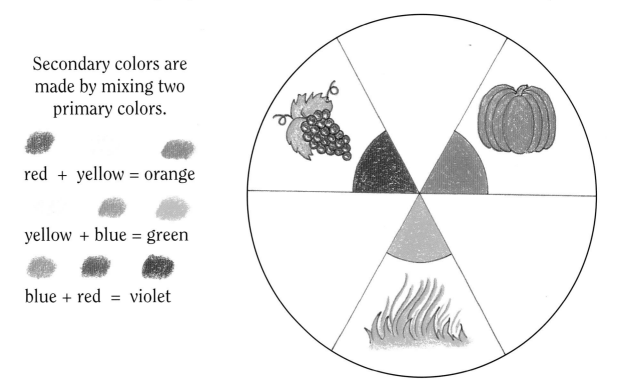

Learn more about North America...

HOW DO FARMS AND CITIES AFFECT FORESTS?   Page 36

*Forests are cleared of trees and bushes to make way for farmland crops and city buildings.
Follow the life of a town and the river beside it in* A RIVER RAN WILD *written and illustrated
by Lynne Cherry, published by Harcourt Brace Jovanovich, 1992.*

WHAT OTHER PLANTS GROW IN THE INTERIOR?   Page 39

*Wheat, corn, oats and other farm crops now cover much of this vast region. For a look at what rural life
is like on the Interior's fertile plains,* read A PRAIRIE ALPHABET *by Jo Bannatyne-Cugnet, illustrated by
Yvette Moore, published by Tundra Books, 1992.*

CAN YOU FIND THE MOUNTAIN RANGES OF NORTH AMERICA ON A MAP?   Page 40

*Look for the Rocky Mountains and Appalachians. Can you name the smaller ranges? Are the mountains
in the East as tall as the western mountains? Visit a range in* SIERRA *by Diane Siebert, illustrated by
Wendell Minor, published by HarperCollins, 1991.*

WHAT HAPPENS WHEN IT RAINS ON THE DESERT?   Page 43

It's an event! Even the toads celebrate in the wake of the thunderstorm that sweeps through the desert in
IT RAINED ON THE DESERT TODAY *by Ken and Debby Buchanan, illustrated by Libba Tracy, published
by Northland Publishing, 1994.*

WHAT IS THE TUNDRA?   Page 44

*The tundra is cold—so cold that all but the top layer of the ground stays frozen even in the summer. Can
anything live or grow here? Yes! See* ONE SMALL SQUARE: ARCTIC TUNDRA *by Donald Silver, illustrated
by Patricia Wynne, published by Freeman, 1994.*

READ MORE ABOUT NORTH AMERICA!

O CANADA *written and illustrated by Ted Harrison, published by Houghton Mifflin, 1993. Read about
Canada's landscapes and cultures while touring the Canadian provinces. Explore the New Brunswick
forest, learn about the French-speaking people of Quebec, meet the cowboys of Alberta and marvel over
the northern lights of the Yukon!*

PADDLE-TO-THE-SEA *written and illustrated by Holling Clancy Holling, published by Houghton Mifflin,
1941. Learn about the Great Lakes while following the journey of a boy's model canoe.*

AMERICA THE BEAUTIFUL *by Katharine Lee Bates, illustrated by Neil Waldman, published by Macmillan,
1993. The words of a familiar song come alive with paintings of places such as Niagara Falls, the Napa
Valley of California and an ancient cliff dwelling.*

WHERE THE BUFFALO ROAM *adapted and illustrated by Jacqueline Geis, published by Hambleton-
Hill, 1992. Again, a familiar song and artwork highlight a part of this continent—the Southwest of the
United States. Bet you can't keep from singing along!*

COUNT YOUR WAY THROUGH MEXICO *by Jim Haskins, illustrated by Helen Byers, published by
Carolrhoda, 1989. Learn about Mexico—a country of magnificent ancient cultures, colorful traditions
and beautiful birds and animals.*

The Pilgrims

England's king made laws.
One was to go to his church.
Some people did not like it.
They were the Pilgrims.

Where is England?

The Pilgrims in England

Teaching Tip on page 64
Question answered on page 62

Pilgrim Man   Pilgrim Woman

The Pilgrims in Holland

Teaching Tip on page 64
Question answered on page 62

1.

2.

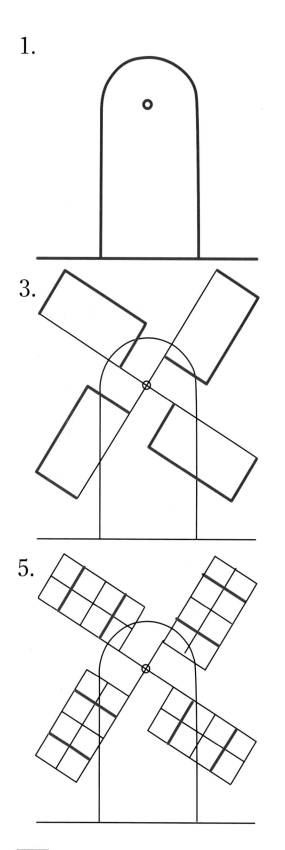

3.

4.

5.

6.

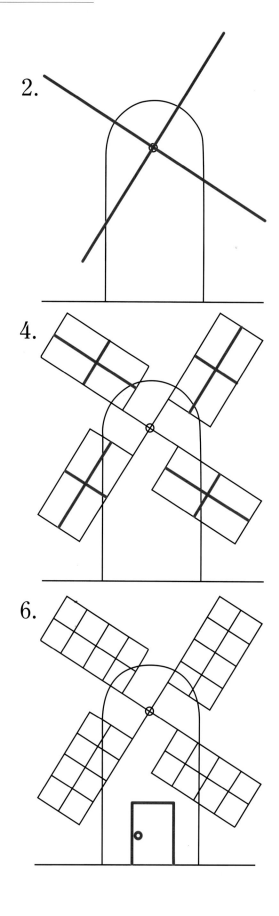

The Pilgrims moved to Holland.
They lived there for 12 years.
Life was hard for them.
They wanted a better life.

Why did
the Pilgrims
move to
Holland?

The Pilgrims sailed to America.
Their ship was the Mayflower.
There were 102 passengers.
They landed in November 1620.

What were ships like in the 1600s?

1.

2.

3.

4.

5.

6.

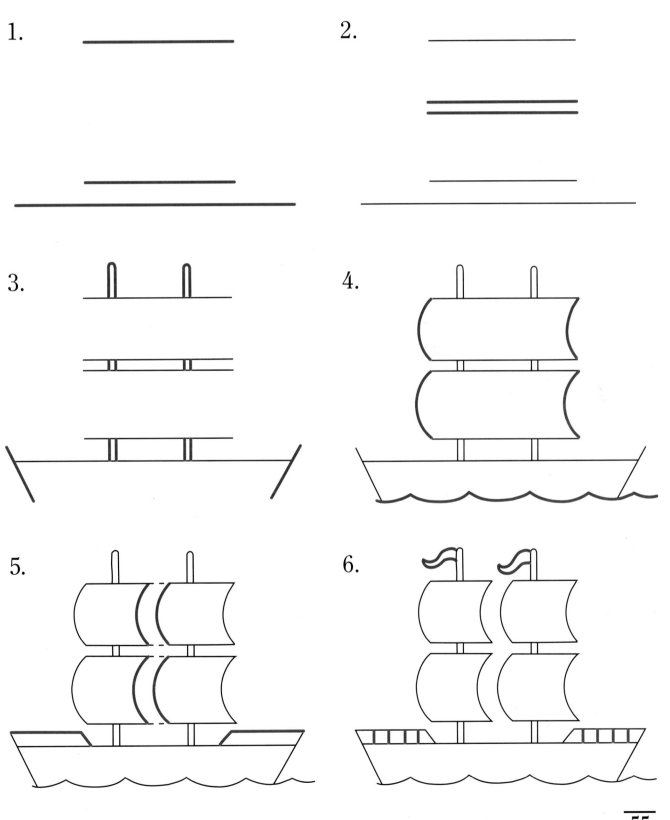

Plymouth

Teaching Tip on page 64
Question answered on page 62

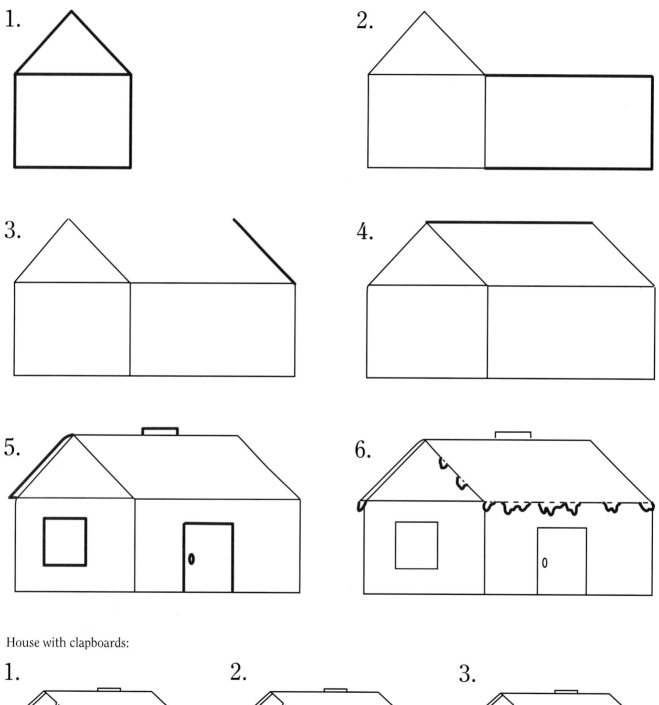

1.

2.

3.

4.

5.

6.

House with clapboards:

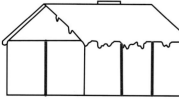

1.

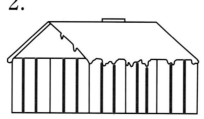

2.

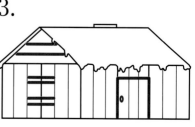

3.

The Pilgrims arrived in winter.
Only a few houses were built.
They named their town Plymouth.
The winter was hard.

Was it difficult to build a town in winter?

Squanto helped the Pilgrims.
He taught them many things.
He showed them how to plant.
Their crops grew well.

Why did Squanto add fish when he planted corn?

Squanto

Question answered on page 62

1.
2.
3.

4.
5.
6.

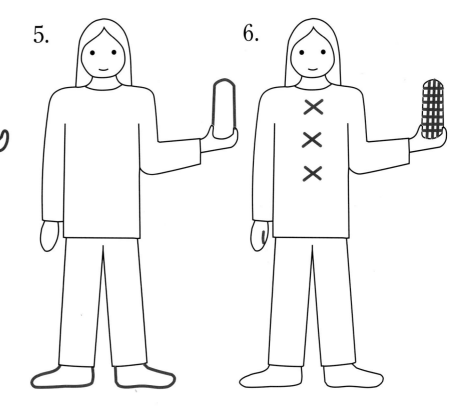

Draw From Your Imagination

Imagine all the colors you can use!

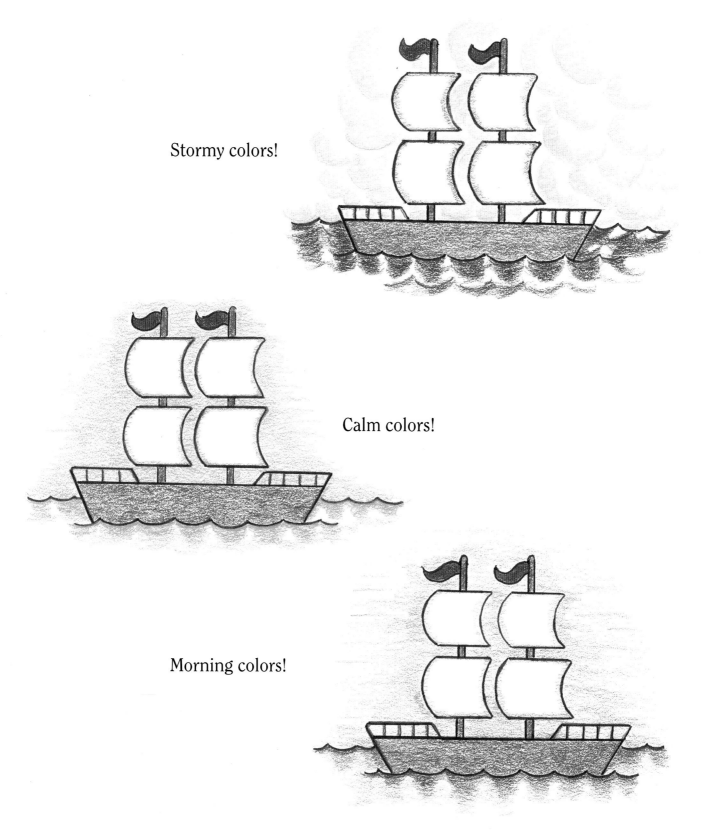

Stormy colors!

Calm colors!

Morning colors!

There are six "intermediate" colors.

Intermediate colors are made by mixing a primary color with a secondary color.

red + orange = red-orange

yellow + orange = yellow-orange

yellow + green = yellow-green

blue + green = blue-green

blue + violet = blue-violet

red + violet = red-violet

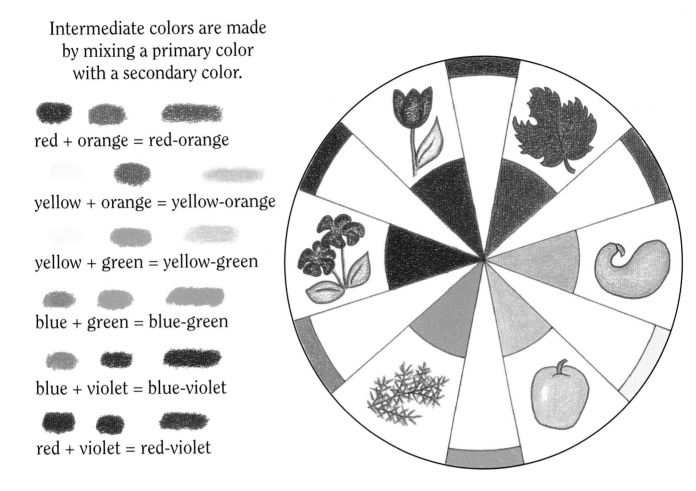

Some colors are warm.

Some colors are cool.

Learn more about the Pilgrims...

WHERE IS ENGLAND?   Page 50

England, part of the United Kingdom, is a small European country with a long world history. The Pilgrims were originally from England. In 1620, 102 people —over 30 of them children—set sail for North America in search of a new home. Read their story in THE PILGRIMS OF PLIMOTH *written and illustrated by Marcia Sewall, published by Athenium, 1986.*

WHY DID THE PILGRIMS MOVE TO HOLLAND?   Page 53

The people of Holland imposed no demands on the Pilgrims to conform to their beliefs or ideals—an unusual concept at that time in Europe. Even so, the Pilgrims were not content in Holland. Read about their years in Holland in chapters 1-4 of MARGARET PUMPHREY'S PILGRIM STORIES *by Elvajean Hall, published by Scholastic, 1991.*

WHAT WERE SHIPS LIKE IN THE 1600s?   Page 54

The ships made by Europeans during the 1600s were sailing ships designed to carry cargo, not passengers. The Pilgrims' voyage aboard the Mayflower was long, crowded and uncomfortable. Read more about the Pilgrims' voyage in IF YOU SAILED ON THE MAYFLOWER IN 1620 *by Ann McGovern, illustrated by Anna DiVito, published by Scholastic, 1991.*

WAS IT DIFFICULT TO BUILD A TOWN IN WINTER?   Page 57

Yes! Building was difficult because winter months in the Northeast are cold and often stormy. Also, the Pilgrims were weak and many of them were sick from their long voyage. See who helped the Pilgrims after that difficult winter of 1620-1621 in THE FIRST THANKSGIVING *by Jean Craighead George, illustrated by Thomas Locker, published by Philomel, 1993.*

WHY DID SQUANTO ADD FISH WHEN HE PLANTED CORN?   Page 58

The people native to the area knew the soil needed fertilizer for corn to grow well. By adding fish, Squanto put important nutrients into the soil. Long before the Pilgrims came, generations of Squanto's people— the Wampanoags—lived in the area. Hear their story in PEOPLE OF THE BREAKING DAY *by Marcia Sewall, published by Athenium, 1990.*

WHAT IS A PILGRIM? A COLONIST? AN IMMIGRANT?

Pilgrims *are people who go on a long journey, usually for religious reasons. A Russian family that immigrated to America many years ago, identifies with the Pilgrims and takes comfort in hearing the Thanksgiving story in* MOLLY'S PILGRIM *by Barbara Cohen, published by Lothrop, Lee & Shepard, 1983.*

Colonists *are people who start a settlement in a land that their country has claimed as its own. One hundred years before the Pilgrims' arrival, Europeans began an explosion in exploration, conquering and trading in the Americas. See how this led to colonization in* EXPLORATION AND CONQUEST *by Betsy and Giulio Maestro, published by Lothrop, Lee & Shepard, 1994.*

Immigrants *are people who are welcomed into a country and make it their home. Follow the voyage of one group of immigrants in* HOW MANY DAYS TO AMERICA? *by Eve Bunting, illustrated by Beth Peck, published by Houghton Mifflin, 1988.*

Teaching Tips

PUEBLO (page 24) — To make this picture simpler, have the children draw the pueblo two dimensionally. Omit the vertical lines in step 5 and the horizontal lines in step 6.

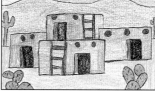

by Ali Garrett, age 7

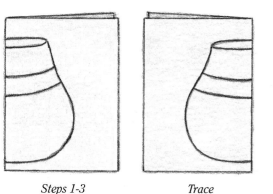

Steps 1-3   *Trace*

POTS AND BASKETS (page 27) — Some children may become frustrated if their drawings are not symmetrical. If this is the case, have them fold their papers in half. Have each child draw one-half of a container (steps 1-3). With their papers still folded and working from the opposite side, have the children trace the lines they have drawn. If their papers are too heavy to see through, hold them against a light source such as a window. After drawing their pots or baskets, the children can unfold their papers to decorate their containers.

North America

THE INTERIOR—SUNFLOWER (page 38) — The sunflower's petals are spaced evenly around the flower's center. The guidelines shown in steps 1-3 will help the children space their petals. The sunflower's petals are also the same length (steps 2, 3 and 4). To help the children draw their petals the same length, draw a large outer circle on their papers as a guide. Another option is to provide each child with round paper on which to draw a flower head. The children can then paste their flower heads to another sheet of paper on which they have drawn stems, leaves and backgrounds.

THE WEST—EAGLE (page 41) — Each of the eagle's wings is about as long as its head, body and tail. Mention this to the children before starting the lesson. Help the children with the size and placement of the eagle's body (step 1). Consider giving them a pattern of the body to trace. Before adding the wings (step 3), show them how to measure the length of the eagle's head, body and tail with either a ruler or with their hands. Use that measurement as a guide for the length of each wing.

The Pilgrims

THE PILGRIMS IN ENGLAND (page 51) — It takes time to draw both Pilgrims! Give students the option of drawing only one Pilgrim. When teaching this lesson, draw the man and woman simultaneously so that everyone finishes at about the same time.

THE PILGRIMS IN HOLLAND (page 52) — Tulips are fun to draw!

1. 2. 3.

PLYMOUTH (page 56) — The clapboard option gives children practice in dividing spaces into halves and thirds.